坐禪

Zazen

The Essential Guide for Practicing Zen Meditation in the Lotus Position

by Bino Schree

Table of Contents

Introduction 1

Chapter 1: What Is Zen? 7

Chapter 2: Understanding Zazen Rituals 11

Chapter 3: What You'll Need 15

Chapter 4: The Four Ways to Sit 21

Chapter 5: Clothing, Posture, and the Cosmic Mudra 27

Chapter 6: How to Breathe 33

Chapter 7: Putting It All Together 37

Chapter 8: Focusing on Your Breath 41

Conclusion: Why Practice Zazen? 47

Introduction

Zazen is a form of meditation used by a sect of Japanese Buddhists, and is written with two Kanji (Chinese characters adopted in the Japanese writing system) that pretty much describe it all. *Za* (坐) means "to sit," while *Zen* (禪) means "to meditate." Zazen can therefore be understood to mean "sitting meditation" or "to sit in meditation."

The word "Zen" is a much abused word in the English language. Many people use it to describe a form of décor, an architectural and design style, a type of gardening layout, etc.; but none of these things are remotely correct.

The Chinese characters 禪那 are pronounced as *chán-nà* in Mandarin. It was an attempt to transliterate the Sanskrit word *dhyāna*, which means "meditation," since Buddhism originated in India. Today, the Chinese continue to use 禪 as *chán* and have dropped the 那 (*nà*). The Japanese have adopted this convention, but they pronounce 禪 as *Zen*. In case you're wondering, Chinese characters do not depict sound, but meaning.

While certain forms of architecture, décor, design, and gardening can indeed be conducive to meditation, you begin to see how silly it is to describe these things as Zen. So the next time you see your Chinese or Japanese friends roll their eyes at terms like "Zen garden," "Zen decor," "Zen living room," or "that's so Zen," you'll know why.

There are many different schools of Zen, and therefore, many different ways to practice Zazen. There are also many different ways to meditate, as well as many different things to meditate on. This book will provide a basic introduction to Zazen. It will also focus on the four traditional seating methods, as well as the two basic forms of meditation.

It must be pointed out, however, that Zazen isn't just about sitting and meditating. Nor is it really a religion as we understand that word in the West, or about the school you belong to. Zazen is not an objective in itself. Rather it is simply a tool, a means of reaching a goal.

Think of Zen as the bow and Zazen as the arrow. The bow is the guiding theory behind the practice, while Zazen is the arrow which puts that practice into action. The better you understand the bow and the better you control the arrow, the better you'll be at hitting your target. To succeed, however, you'll have to put in the time and the effort. So without further ado, let's get started!

© Copyright 2015 by Miafn LLC - All rights reserved.

This document is geared towards providing reliable information in regards to the topic and issue covered. The publication is sold with the idea that the publisher is not required to render accounting, officially permitted, or otherwise, qualified services. If advice is necessary, legal or professional, a practiced individual in the profession should be ordered.

- From a Declaration of Principles which was accepted and approved equally by a Committee of the American Bar Association and a Committee of Publishers and Associations.

In no way is it legal to reproduce, duplicate, or transmit any part of this document in either electronic means or in printed format. Recording of this publication is strictly prohibited and any storage of this document is not allowed unless with written permission from the publisher. All rights reserved.

The information provided herein is stated to be truthful and consistent, in that any liability, in terms of inattention or otherwise, by any usage or abuse of any policies, processes, or directions contained within is solely and completely the responsibility of the recipient reader. Under no circumstances will any legal responsibility or blame be held against the publisher for any reparation, damages, or monetary loss due to the information herein, either directly or indirectly.

Respective authors own all copyrights not held by the publisher.

The information herein is offered for informational purposes solely, and is universal as so. The presentation of the information is without contract or any type of guarantee assurance.

The trademarks that are used are without any consent, and the publication of the trademark is without permission or backing by the trademark owner. All trademarks and brands within this book are for clarifying purposes only and are the owned by the owners themselves, not affiliated with this document.

Chapter 1: What Is Zen?

Technically speaking, it is a school of thought that belongs to the Mahayana branch of Buddhism. Just as Christians are either Catholics or Protestants, Buddhists are either Theravāda or Mahāyāna. And just as Protestantism is made up of many different and incredibly diverse sects, the same can be said of Mahāyāna.

Centuries after Buddha died, Buddhism became a lot of things to many different people. In time, it no longer reflected the original teachings, especially when some cultures turned Buddha into a god (which he most definitely is not).

Some people tried to get back to the original teachings, but during the Tang Dynasty in China (618-907), they tried a different tactic. Instead of focusing on texts, they decided to instead focus on the meditative practices that Buddha taught.

This bit cannot be emphasized enough, since it forms the entire basis of Zen and Zazen. Buddhism, like all other religions, has its own body of scriptures called the Sutras (aphorisms). These can generally be divided into three:

1) Dictations of the Buddha's teachings, recorded at the time he was still alive

2) The written interpretations of what the Buddha said, according to those students who were actually there with him

3) The interpretations of late followers (often many centuries later)

While those Tang scholars didn't turn their backs on the Sutras or Buddhist doctrine, they decided to instead focus on the common thread that unites all Buddhist schools—the pursuit of nirvāṇa (enlightenment) through meditation.

The different schools can (and do) argue over what the Buddha meant by this or that, but they all agreed on three things:

1) Buddha said that all people should meditate.

2) He left very clear instructions on how this should be done.

3) He said that meditation was an important key to attaining nirvāṇa.

So they called their system *dhyāna*, later *chánnà*, and later still, simply *chán*. This school of thought spread to Vietnam, Korea, and finally Japan, where they called it *Zen*.

This is not to say that Zen has no doctrine, scripture, or rituals. The doctrine focuses on teachings about the value of self-realization, as well as the nature of reality. None of these will be explained here. The rituals, on the other hand, are integral to Zazen.

Zen requires no faith, per se. It has a view of the world, then encourages you to explore the validity of that view or disprove of it through your own practice and self-exploration. And how do you explore it? Through Zazen, of course.

Chapter 2: Understanding Zazen Rituals

Though it literally means "sitting meditation" or "sitting in meditation," there's a lot more involved. Some argue that Zazen is the ritualistic aspect of Zen philosophy, and while this is rather too simplistic, it's not that far off the mark, either.

In Buddhism, rituals aim to remove uncertainty. When you know what the steps are, you can focus on the meditation more smoothly and avoid having to make things up on the spot. Making things up as you go along creates those "oh no, what now?" moments which destroys equanimity.

Think of Zazen rituals as the steps to a dance. Once you know and master those steps, you can avoid having to think about them and simply enjoy the dance.

While strictly focused on sitting meditation, Zazen also dictates how you enter the meditation hall, how you greet others, how you start and end the meditation, whether you face the wall, a scroll or another practitioner, and how you leave the hall.

These will vary from school to school, so those bits won't be covered here.

Zazen's focus is on mindfulness, or more accurately, the understanding that your mind is far more than your identity, habits, and personality. Before you can get there, however, you have to first discipline your mind by becoming conscious of what you're doing, what you're feeling, and what's going on around you on a moment-to-moment basis.

This is also why Zazen has a specific set of instructions on how you sit, what you sit on, and what you do while sitting. It also dictates what you must do and think at the end of your session.

Successfully performing these rituals will not bring you good luck, ward off sickness, or get you a promotion. The steps may be thought of as mental guideposts that you can tick off in your mind. Each time you do them properly, you know you're getting closer and closer to what you need to accomplish.

When done regularly, the rituals also help to get you into the proper frame of mind needed to meditate. Think of the pre-meditation rituals as a warm-up prior to physical exercise, and the post rituals as the sort of cool down you need to do after a workout.

When performing these rituals, it is important to focus on what you're doing at each and every step, making each and every act a form of meditation in itself. Your meditation, in other words, begins before you sit, and continues long after you're done.

With enough practice, you can get into the spirit of things, but if it takes a while, don't be too hard on yourself. In Zazen, as with all things, you have to assume an attitude of humility, patience, forgiveness (including self-forgiveness), non-judgmentalism, and a spirit of letting-go.

Chapter 3: What You'll Need

While it's best to attend an actual Zazen center to receive instructions, there are a lot of things you can do on your own. It also helps to have the right tools. Most places will not have chairs, but Zazen was not invented with Westerners in mind. So let's cover that bit first.

CHAIR

If you're not comfortable sitting on the floor in the lotus posture for long periods of time, use a chair—but be sure to pick one without a back and without arms. The need to constantly adjust your posture is an important part of the meditation, so having something to support your back is a no-no. Arm rests will also get in the way of your arms, which have to be held in a certain way.

If you do suffer from spinal injuries, however, pick one with a straight back. You may also put a cushion behind you to make sure your spine curves a bit for maximum comfort. Whatever you choose, be sure to keep both feet flat on the floor. Do not cross your legs because this will unbalance you, can cause one leg to fall asleep, or both.

ZABUTON

Japanese floor cushions are called zabutons and are a marvel of engineering. Unlike other cushions which are stuffed with foam or feathers, zabutons maintain their shape for many years. This is because of how they're stuffed. They take a very long piece of cloth then fold it again and again till it's about 2 to 3 inches thick. Then they stuff that into a square pillow case (usually around 20"X20" to 30"X30" wide) and sew it shut.

The great thing about zabutons is that they never sag. What this means for you is that wherever you sit on it, you'll never get unbalanced due to uneven thickness. What it means for your bottom is that it'll never sink into an uneven spot and get sore or fall asleep. When it comes to sitting comfortably on the floor for long periods, zabutons are your best friends.

Do note, however, that not all zabutons are made equal. Cheap, mass produced ones, made by a certain non-Japanese country we need not mention, are simply no good. It's best to pick one out yourself, pinching and prodding to make sure it maintains its shape at all points of the cushion. Zabutons are firm when flat, but if you stand them on an edge, they'll fold and fall. They're also quite heavy.

ZAFU

Some people are not entirely comfortable sitting on a zabuton for long periods, so another thing you might want to get is a round, puffy cushion called a zafu. These look like poufs, are usually 14" in diameter and around 8" high, and are stuffed with kapok or buckwheat hulls. This makes them heavier than a regular, foam-stuffed cushion, but they maintain their shape better so you don't end up sinking, or leaning to one side or the other. Zafus are placed atop zabutons so that they raise your buttocks and put less pressure on your knees.

SEIZA

If you've ever seen how some Japanese sit, you might have noticed that some of them rest their upper body on their lower legs. While some can do this unaided, others cheat by using a zafu or by resorting to a wooden bench called a seiza.

Seizas are small, narrow benches long enough to accommodate the length of your buttocks, but not the width. They also tilt and look like lecterns. Placed on a zabuton, the person kneels, rests their butt on the seiza, then puts their lower legs behind them on either side of the seiza. Some seizas are built higher, allowing you to fold your lower legs beneath them.

In lieu of a seiza or zafu, you can also use a thick cushion to support your buttocks so you can maintain a kneeling position for extended periods more comfortably. Experiment to see what works best for you.

ZAISU

If you need back support for your zabuton, this is a must. Zaisus are L-shaped backrests. You place the lower leg of the "L" beneath the zabuton and lean back on the upper portion, though some zaisus come with their own non-detachable zabuton. While not generally encouraged for Zazen, it's fine if you're starting out or if you have back problems.

Chapter 4: The Four Ways to Sit

In Zazen, comfort is very important. You therefore have to find a posture that you can maintain for long periods without moving, fidgeting, shifting, or readjusting your position. Experiment with the following to see what works best for you. Please note that unless you choose to sit on a chair, all positions are to be done on a zabuton (or other well-padded mattress) for comfort.

SEIZA

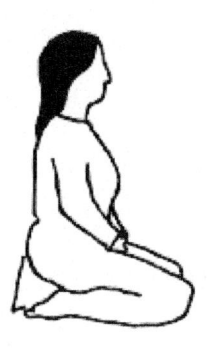

This requires the use of a zafu or a seiza bench. If you do use the latter, please note that it doesn't usually work on a regular cushion. Zabutons are great at taking the weight of a seiza bench, but other cushions tend to deflate beneath the pressure of one. If your cushion is too thick, the pressure of the seiza will lower the back, forcing you to tilt forward to compensate. Thin cushions are ideal for seiza benches, but their thinness can eventually cause your knees and shin to hurt.

Do not support your buttocks with either a high seiza or zafu. In Zazen, you have to rest your folded hands on your lap before your groin. If you elevate your buttocks too much, you will have to work harder to keep your hands in place, which can cause strain on your shoulders and lower arms.

This is why you should give your seiza or zafu a test run. Most stores allow it, but that's rather hard to do if you order one online.

BURMESE

This is best done with a zafu. In this posture, you sit with your butt elevated, but don't use a seiza because the tilt of the bench will cause you to slide forward. Stick with a flat-surfaced cushion for maximum balance and comfort.

The tops of both your feet should rest flat on the floor, so that the soles face up, while the left foot rests in front of the right. Your knees should jut out on either side of you, such that both your heels point toward your groin. This is the ideal position. An alternative is to rest one foot in front of the other calf, or in front of the other knee, whichever is most comfortable for you.

You will not rest one leg over the other in this posture. Your legs will form a triangle beneath you, not in front of you as with the lotus posture.

HALF LOTUS

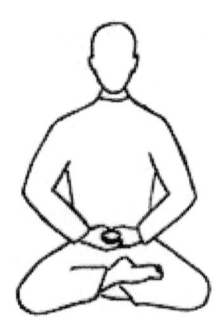

Half lotus means you keep your right leg folded beneath your upper left leg while resting your lower left foot on your right thigh. You can also reverse that, if you prefer.

When assuming this position, however, take care not to rest one ankle over the other, as this will make both legs fall asleep. Also avoid resting the top leg over your lower calf for the same reason. The best place to rest the upper leg is on the gap between your lower calf and just above the meaty part of your ankle before it flares out to the calf.

An alternative is to sit this way with an extra cushion beneath your buttocks. You'll still be sitting on a zafu (ideally), but the extra support beneath your butt will make it easier to sit upright. Again be careful not to use too high a cushion.

FULL LOTUS

The yogis and Zen teachers consider this the most ideal position. According to yogic theory, full lotus increases energy and focus, while some Zen masters believe that this was the posture Buddha sat in when he discovered the truth.

While most people can do this, not everyone can maintain it comfortably for long periods. So go with what you can comfortably maintain and not with what the Buddha allegedly did. In this posture, you sit cross legged, rest your left foot on your right thigh, and your right foot on your left thigh.

As with half lotus, you can also place a cushion beneath your butt to help you maintain an upright posture. Do note, however, that in full lotus, the pressure placed on your legs and knees increases further.

Chapter 5: Clothing, Posture, and the Cosmic Mudra

CLOTHING

Clothes should be loose so as not to cut off circulation in any part of your body. Jeans are a bad idea as they bunch up around the back of your knees when you fold your legs. That bunching up can eventually cut off circulation in your lower legs.

You want clothes that are comfortable and loose. Tight waistbands are another bad idea, as are overly wide belts that can upset your stomach because they can dig into your abdomen.

Shoes are never worn during Zazen, nor slippers. If you ever make your way into a meditation hall, you will have to leave your shoes at the entrance. It is considered the height of rudeness to wear shoes inside a Zen temple, as shoes bring the dirt of the outside into a place of purity.

All private and group Zazen sessions are done either barefoot or with socks.

POSTURE

However you choose to sit, try to wiggle your butt out as far behind you as possible. Ridiculous as that sounds, the last thing you want to do is sit on the end bones of your butt—what doctors call the coccyx. By wiggling your butt cheeks out, you manage to rest on the edge, and not on the point, of the bones in your buttocks. You might want to sway about from side to side to make sure that you're perfectly balanced and comfortable.

If you choose a chair, make sure you have a cushion beneath you, but not one that's too thick lest you get unbalanced. This is a lot trickier if you use a zafu, but should be a piece of cake with a seiza.

Once you manage to push your buttocks behind you in a way that's comfortable, you'll have to lean forward slightly. Compensate by leaning your shoulders back a little, creating a very slight arch in the middle of your spine. Your shoulders should rest comfortably on that arch.

If you choose to lean against a chair's back or a zaisu, be careful not to put too much weight on your buttocks. If your coccyx hurts a little, it'll hurt a lot more before the session is over, so feel free to make whatever adjustments you have to till you're as comfortable as possible.

Now pay attention to your belly. Your upright position should not interfere with your breathing. If you feel a slight crease on your stomach, you're probably leaning forward a little. If you feel a slight tension there, then you're probably leaning back too much.

HEAD

Your head should face-forward, such that your lower jaw lies parallel to the floor. Do not tilt your head forward or backward, so as not to constrict your throat and affect your breathing. Imagine having a string attached to the top of your head (like that of a puppet) to keep your head perfectly upright and facing straight ahead.

EYES OPEN

Zen contains two characters, 礻 and 單. The latter contains two small squares on top, representing two open eyes atop a body. This is because unlike most forms of sitting meditation, you have to keep your eyes open.

You are not to open your eyes wide, only keep them halfway open. Some focus their gaze on the tips of their nose, while others on a blank wall or on a spot on the floor a few inches away from them. Another option is to just keep your eyes slightly open and let your gaze remain unfocused.

Whatever you do with your eyes, make sure they're relaxed and looking downward. Looking up or straight ahead puts strain on your eyes, which is the last thing you want.

THE COSMIC MUDRA

Mudras are hand gestures believed to invoke certain powers, as well as put you in a certain frame of mind. The cosmic mudra is said to help direct people's minds inward, improve intuition and insight, as well as suppress wandering thoughts.

If you are right-handed, open your hand, place it palm up before your groin, and rest your right wrist on your upper thigh. Now open your left palm and place it palm up so that the fingers rest on those below. The tips of your thumbs should meet above. If you are left-handed, place your left hand on the lower position and the right on top.

Do note, however, that some schools don't care what your dominant hand is. They dictate the positioning based on their own tradition.

Chapter 6: How to Breathe

This is the trickiest for beginners to master, but until you get it right, you can't meditate properly. All forms of meditation use diaphragmatic breathing, meaning you breathe only with your belly, not with your chest.

If you pay attention to how you breathe, you'll notice that your shoulders rise and fall and that your chest moves. This is an inefficient way to breathe because it does not maximize oxygen intake, nor does it effectively expel toxins.

While breathing with your chest is great for bursts of energy, such as when you're running, it is not a good way to relax. Nor should you make a habit of it. To develop diaphragmatic breathing, it might help to sit in front of a mirror—one big enough so you can see your chest and tummy.

Exhale, spread your fingers apart, and place your palms flat on your tummy. The tips of your middle fingers should meet over your belly button. Relax your shoulders and chest, and do your best not to move them.

Now inhale, taking care to bring the breath all the way down into your tummy. Your fingers should spread and the tips of your middle fingers should pull apart.

Exhale by pulling your stomach in. The tips of your middle fingers should again touch.

If your shoulders still rise and fall, practice your breathing till your shoulders and chest no longer move. Only your tummy should expand and contract.

Even when you're not sitting in meditation, pay attention to your breathing throughout the day. If you catch yourself feeling stressed and breathing shallowly with your chest, take a moment to relax and consciously practice breathing only with your tummy. Whenever stress catches up with you, do this exercise. It'll do wonders for you.

Chapter 7: Putting It All Together

Some people use a bell to start and end meditation, but unless you're in a meditation hall or with a group, it's not necessary. Zazen should be a daily practice done on an empty stomach, which is why it's traditionally done before breakfast, or three hours after a meal.

REGULARITY

When choosing a spot for Zazen, it's best to pick a place where you won't be disturbed for at least ten to fifteen minutes. A quiet, private, and out of the way spot is ideal. And be sure to turn off your phone.

It's also best to pick the same time each day, if possible. Meditating at the same time and in the same place is a great way to condition your mind and body for what's to come.

SANCTITY

Traditionally, the tools you use (zabuton, zafu, seiza, etc.) are only for Zazen and nothing else. This way, you associate them specifically with your meditation practice. Doing so imbues them with a sense of sanctity.

Let's go back to the character 禪, which is made up of 礻 (shi) and 單 (tan). While the second one can represent an upright person with two open eyes on top (it doesn't, but it's great for demonstration purposes), the 礻 means "altar."

Put together, the character suggests that meditation is a sacred act and should therefore be treated accordingly. You don't need an altar, but by devoting your tools only for Zazen, you create a sacred space, one that is special and different from your normal, mundane world.

MINDFULNESS

Once you walk into your Zazen spot, pay attention to everything you do, how your body feels, how it moves, how your clothes feel as you move, what the temperature in the room is like, how you're breathing, etc. This is called mindfulness. The aim is not to be in automatic mode, but to stay as keenly aware of everything around you as you possibly can.

1) Tradition dictates that you bow to your zabuton (or chair) before you sit on it, but that's entirely up to you.

2) Mindfully sit down.

3) Spend a minute or two finding the position that feels the most comfortable and that you're sure you can maintain without moving.

4) Place your hands on your lap and assume the cosmic mudra.

5) Now breathe diaphragmatically.

Chapter 8: Focusing on Your Breath

Making breath your sole focus is the point of Zazen.

There are two methods involved, but in both, you should keep your jaw relaxed and your mouth slightly open. Keep your lips shut and lightly rest the tip of your tongue behind your upper teeth. Doing so suppresses saliva so you won't have to be distracted by swallowing and/or clearing your throat.

NATURAL BREATHING

As its name implies, simply breathe in and out diaphragmatically. Try to be as natural and as comfortable as you can. In the beginning, it might also help you to focus on:

1) How your tummy moves in and out

2) Maintaining an upright and comfortable posture

Your primary focus, however, should be on your breathing.

COUNTING BREATH

This is also called equalizing the breath.

It still requires diaphragmatic breathing, but instead of just breathing in and out, do so with a regular count. As you breathe in, do so for a slow and regular count of five, and as you breathe out, do so for the same count. There will be a brief pause between each in-breath and out-breath, but it should be a comfortable pause, not a prolonged one.

If you devote ten minutes to your practice, for example, spend the first two minutes doing natural breathing. Then begin counting your breath. After eight minutes, get back to breathing normally for the last two minutes of your session.

ITCHINESS OR DISCOMFORT

If you feel an itch, don't scratch. There's always some part of you that itches, but because your mind is usually distracted, you often don't notice. Now that you're focusing your mind, you'll notice them. By keeping your attention on your in-breath and out-breath, itchiness usually goes away eventually.

If the itch persists, keep your primary focus on your breathing and let a small part of you locate the itch. Mentally observe the itch. Is it focused or diffuse? Is it intense or mild? Do not get emotionally involved in the itch by getting irritated or by scratching right away. Simply accept that these things happen, but keep your primary focus on your breathing.

If the itch just won't go away, then mindfully scratch it while keeping your primary focus on your breath. Your goal is to observe your mind and how it reacts to things, not react automatically to feelings and impulses.

Your ultimate goal is to master your body with your mind, and not let your body be the master of your mind. But be patient and start with your breath.

IMPATIENCE

At some point, you'll wonder why you're sitting there and not doing something more productive. This is natural, but is again an emotional reaction. Deal with discomfort and other mental distractions as you would an itch.

THOUGHTS and DISTRACTIONS

Suppressing thoughts is useless, especially in the beginning. Let them come, but do not engage them. If you remember an appointment, for example, let that thought arise, but do not engage in mental chatter. Don't go, "Oh no, I should call…" Just acknowledge that you have an appointment and keep your primary focus on your breathing.

ENDING

When you're through, a simple bow, done mindfully, signals the end. In a hall or with a group, the leader usually rings a bell. Get up mindfully and go about your day, but try to maintain that sense of mindfulness by bringing your attention back to your breath whenever you can.

Conclusion: Why Practice Zazen?

There's a lot of information out there on the mental and physical benefits of meditation, so it won't be covered here. Whether you choose to go to a Zen center or take up another form of meditation, is completely irrelevant.

The exercises described in this book form the basis of all types of meditation. You can do away with zabutons and zafus, as well as the cosmic mudra.

But breath is life, so paying attention to your breath is a guaranteed way of developing focus and concentration. While it can seem like a waste of time, consider how much of it you waste on your own, anyway.

If you do Zazen regularly, you'll notice that your mind eventually becomes calm. Rather than doing things automatically, you'll realize that a lot of things you think and feel are fleeting, impermanent, and unimportant.

You are not your habits, your thoughts, or your feelings. Nor are you a mere animal doomed to give in to impulses. You don't have to be like Pavlov's dog, salivating each time it hears a bell even when it's neither hungry nor thirsty.

You are something else far greater, far wiser, and far more powerful.

Zazen practice breaks your conditioning by making you aware of just how much of your life is spent in automatic mode. The more you realize that, the freer you are to become your true amazing self.

Finally, I'd like to thank you for purchasing this book! If you enjoyed it or found it helpful, I'd greatly appreciate it if you'd take a moment to leave a review on Amazon. Thank you!

Printed in Great Britain
by Amazon